ART TRICKS

PRACTICE SKETCH PAD